James D. Reed
A gift for

Great grandma "Thelma"
From

Bee
Happy

Honey from My Heart
for You, Grandchild

Illustrated by Debra Jordan Bryan

COUNTRYMAN

Published by J Countryman
A division of Thomas Nelson, Inc.,
Nashville, Tennessee 37214

Project Editor—Terri Gibbs

Designed by Left Coast Design,
Portland, Oregon

ISBN: 0-8499-9532-9

www.jcountryman.com
www.thomasnelson.com

Printed in China

Today's
assignment:
BEE Happy!!

Bee
Happy

Tomorrow's assignment:

Kiss mom and dad daily.

Say your prayers.

Stay out of trouble.

_____

_____

_____

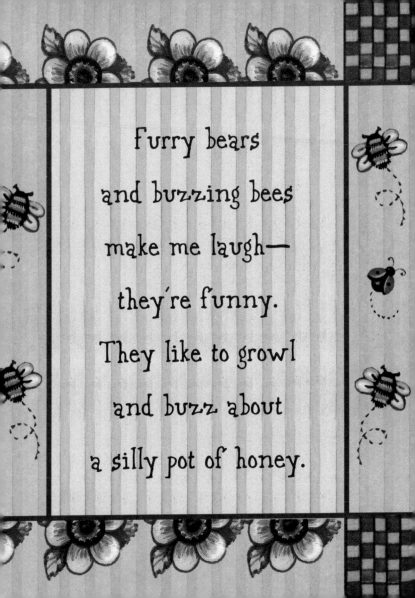

Furry bears
and buzzing bees
make me laugh—
they're funny.
They like to growl
and buzz about
a silly pot of honey.

The day is
much more
friendly when
I can spend it
with you.

Some of my favorite things to do with you:

Make you tickle

Talk to you since I'm not near you.

Watch you grow.

All things
grow with
love . . .
and honey.

A little prayer for you:

Father in Heaven,

Take care of J.D. and his

family — Keep them in your care.

Thank you — in Jesus
name "Amen"

The bees make
sweet honey,
and you make
life sunny!

Bee 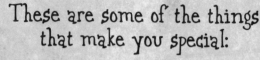 Good

These are some of the things that make you special:

You're my great grand -

You're so sweet -

You're a blessing

You're your mom's

mom only grand

You are handsome

as Devin say's you're fine

Bee Kind

Nothing
makes me smile
like a happy
thought of you!

Someone to love you,
someone to hug you . . .

someone to say,
"You'll BEE okay."
That is honey for the heart!

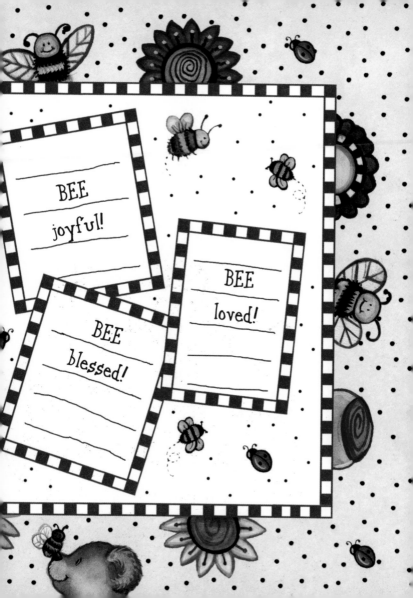

Here's a hug
from my heart,
just to let you know . . .

I love you
BEARY
MUCH!!!

Great grand, Thelma